MW01492419

Bryn Mawr Latin Commentaries

Editors

Julia Haig Gaisser
Bryn Mawr College

James J. O'Donnell
University of Pennsylvania

The purpose of the Bryn Mawr Latin Commentaries is to make a wide range of classical and post-classical authors accessible to the intermediate student. Each commentary provides the minimum grammatical and lexical information necessary for a first reading of the text.

Bryn Mawr Latin Commentaries

Nepos
Dion

Grace Starry West

Thomas Library
Bryn Mawr College

The Bryn Mawr Latin Commentaries
are supported by a generous grant from the
Division of Education Programs of the
National Endowment for the Humanities

Acknowledgments

I would like to thank the University of Dallas for awarding me a Faculty Study Stipend in summer, 1985, which made it possible for me to revise this commentary. The stipend was part of a larger award from the National Endowment for the Humanities to enable the faculty of the University of Dallas to study and improve the teaching of courses in the core curriculum. I also thank my colleagues who have used the commentary in their classes and have made valuable suggestions for its improvement: Rev. Placid Csizmazia, O. Cist., and Mr. Michael Cusick. Finally, thanks are due to the editor of the series, Julia Haig Gaisser, for her comments and corrections. Any errors remaining are of course my own.

G.S.W.
13 November 1985

Introduction

Cornelius Nepos is an ethical biographer, for he seeks to show the character of his subjects through their actions. Because he sometimes bends facts the better to reveal character, he has in modern times earned the reputation of a careless biographer and an indifferent historian. But this assessment misses Nepos' point. Through the arrangement and details in his narrative of the lives of particular men, Nepos raises for us abiding questions of human existence that affect all men. Taken as a whole, the book of which **Dion** is a part, **De excellentibus ducibus exterarum gentium (Outstanding Leaders of Foreign Nations)** encourages us, as it did Nepos' Roman contemporaries, to look beyond our own time and place for answers to questions about leadership. We see what a good leader is, what trials he faces, what virtues he brings to meet the trials, and also, since perfection is impossible, by what deficiencies of character and temperament or vicissitudes of fortune he is plagued. That Nepos chose to raise these questions quietly, relying on his readers to draw them forth from his apparently simple narratives, is perhaps due to a strong desire for survival as much as to literary taste. Born in Cisalpine Gaul about 99 B.C., Nepos lived during a period of constant political turmoil in Rome. He appears to have taken no direct part in politics and to have died in 24 B.C., presumably of old age, more than 15 years after the proscription and murder of Cicero, his flamboyant contemporary and acquaintance.

Dion is the tenth of twenty-three biographies contained in **Outstanding Leaders** (or **Generals**) **of Foreign Nations**, which is in turn the only complete part of a much larger work, **De viris illustribus (Illustrious Men)**. Although Hellenistic Greek biographers of the third and second centuries B.C. are sure to have written collections of biographies along similar lines, Nepos' collection, in Latin, is the earliest to survive. In contrast to the Hellenistic biographers but perhaps following his older Roman contemporary Varro, Nepos conceived his **De viris illustribus** as a means of comparing the Romans with the Greeks, although lives of a few Persians and Carthaginians (e.g. Hannibal) were included. The work contained at least sixteen books, arranged in eight thematic pairs; the first book of each pair dealt with outstanding foreigners, the second with Romans. In addition to generals, categories of historians, kings, and poets are known for a certainty. For the other four, scholars have suggested philosophers, statesmen, orators, and grammarians. Two Roman lives are extant, one of the Elder Cato, the other of Nepos' intimate friend Atticus. In conception, then, the **Parallel Lives** of Plutarch, a Greek who wrote fifty years or so after Nepos, owe much to Nepos' **De viris illustribus.**

Other works of Nepos that are completely lost to us include **Chronica,** a history of the world to Nepos' own times; **Exempla,** anecdotes; a work on geography; and lives of Cato and Cicero separate from **De viris illustribus.**

Cornelius Nepos' Dion

Nepos' Dion is a brilliant general who frees his city Syracuse from a fifty-year tyranny but quickly turns to tyrannous actions in his own attempts to govern and is murdered within four years by the would-be tyrant Callicrates, a man he considered his close friend. The general questions raised by the "plot" of the biography, then, concern tyrants as leaders and tyranny as a regime.

The central question, however, concerns Dion's character. Although he acts like a tyrant, is he a tyrant? Why did Dion, so excellent by nature and by education, come to so bad an end? Is **fortuna** (section 6.1) really responsible for Dion's downfall, as Nepos appears to claim, and do nature and teaching thus have little consequence in men's lives? Since Nepos rarely expresses his opinion, and then only in a general way, the reader must pay close attention to the organization of the narrative as a whole. For example, Dion's actions and emotions in sections 6-8 may cause us to reassess the importance Nepos seems to give **fortuna,** and in fact to revise our earlier understanding of Dion's character.

Nepos' account of Dion's life agrees in the main with those of the other ancient sources (see **Bibliography**). Partly in the interest of brevity, Nepos frequently omits details, usually found in the more fulsome Plutarch, which would make his narrative easier to follow. Some of these omissions, however, point to a difference in emphasis. Nepos' narrative is a continuous, logically consistent whole focusing on Dion's potential excellences, his efforts to moderate the tyrannies of Dionysius I and Dionysius II, his liberation of Syracuse, his fall from popularity through immoderate speeches and actions, the foolish trust in Callicrates that leads to his death, and his honor as a liberator after his death. This last is apparently not historical, however satisfying it may be to our moral sense.

Most modern assessments of Dion, relying on Plato and Plutarch more than Nepos, conclude that Dion failed at Syracuse because the Syracusans distrusted his family connection with tyrants and preferred a popular democracy to the "philosopher-kingship," i.e. moderate oligarchy, that Dion intended to institute. In this view Dion was defeated by circumstances beyond his control. Nepos' **Dion** conveys a different teaching, which is nonetheless congruent with Plato's own advice (near the end of his **Fourth Letter**) to Dion to be more obliging, for popularity is the means to achievement. Dion's severity toward his son, his disastrous quotation of Homer, the Syracusans' fear of him after Heraclides'

murder, and his proscription of both friends and enemies
(all reported by Nepos but omitted by the other sources)
locate Dion's failure in his own temperament and conse-
quent actions. Nepos' **Dion** is a brief argument through
example that character is of great importance in deter-
mining a man's **fortuna** and, finally, his fate.

Greek Tyranny

Although tyranny (illegal monarchy) had by and large
ceased in the cities of mainland Greece and Ionia by the
early 5th century B.C., it continued longer and recurred
more often in the Greek cities of Sicily. Constant
competition for control of the island with the
Carthaginians and a hostile native population perhaps
contributed to the instability of aristocratic and de-
mocratic governments. The democracy which had
replaced the original aristocratic (or oligarchic)
government of Syracuse (founded ca. 734 B.C. by
Corinthians) soon gave way to the tyrannies of Gelon and
his brother Hieron (485-466). The second period of
tyranny was that of Dionysius I and Dionysius II (406-
357). Still later, an oligarchic government established by
Timoleon (d. ca. 334) was replaced by the tyranny of
Agathocles (317). Thereafter Syracusan politics
depended on the will of Rome.

Bibliography

Cornelius Nepos

1) Texts and Commentaries

Cornelii Nepotis Vitae cum Fragmentis. Ed. Peter K. Marshall. Leipzig, 1977.

Cornelius Nepos. Commentary by K. Nipperdey and K. Witte. 12th ed., Berlin, 1962. Latin text with introduction and commentary (grammatical and historical) in German.

Cornelius Nepos. **Alcibiades, Dion, Atticus.** Introduction and commentary by R. Roebuck. London, 1976.

Cornelius Nepos. Translated by J. C. Rolfe. (Cambridge, Mass., 1929) Latin text; introduction and translation in English.

Cornelii Nepotis Vitae. Ed. E. O. Winstedt. Oxford, 1904. This is the text reprinted in this volume by permission of Oxford University Press.

2) Studies. Although no specific studies of Dion are available in English, the following give some idea in general of Nepos' manner of writing:

Jeffries, J. D. "The Concept of **Fortuna** in Cornelius Nepos," **Classical Philology** 38 (1943) 48-50.

Jenkinson, Edna M. "Nepos. An Introduction to Latin Biography," in **Latin Biography,** ed. T. A. Dorey (New York, 1967), 1-15.

Jenkinson, Edna M., "Cornelius Nepos and the Early History of Biography at Rome," **Aufstieg und Niedergang der Römischen Welt** 1.3 (Tübingen, 1973) 703-19.

Momigliano, A. D. **The Development of Greek Biography** (Cambridge, Mass., 1971), 96-9, 103-4. A brief but unusually positive evaluation of Nepos' achievements.

Dion of Syracuse

Diodorus Siculus. Translated by C. L. Sherman (Cambridge, Mass., 1952) vol. 7. Greek text with English translation. Diodorus flourished under Caesar and Augustus; he continued his universal history to his own times. For Dion see index.

Hackforth, R. "Sicily, 367 to 330 B.C." in **Cambridge Ancient History,** ed. J.B. Bury et al. (Cambridge, 1953) vol. 6, 272-301.

Plato. **Epistles.** Translated by R. G. Bury (Cambridge, Mass., 1961) Greek text with English translation. See particularly Letters 1-4, 7-8, and 13.

Plutarch. **Lives.** Translated by B. Perrin (Cambridge, Mass., 1961), vol. 7, containing P.'s life of Dion. Greek text with English translation.

Woodhead, A. G. **The Greeks in the West** (New York, 1962) See especially chapter 4, 72-114.

N.B.: In the commentary, **AG** refers to Allen and Greenough's **New Latin Grammar** (Boston, 1903, and frequent reprints).

Chronology of Dion of Syracuse

ca. 408 B.C.	Dion is born in Syracuse to Hipparinus, an aristocrat and associate of Dionysius I.
403?	Dionysius I marries Aristomache, Dion's sister.
ca. 387	Dion becomes a pupil of Plato when he visits Syracuse.
?	Dion marries his niece, Arete.
ca. 367	Dionysius I dies; Dionysius II succeeds him.
366?	Plato's second visit; Dion is exiled and settles in Athens.
ca. 361	Plato's third visit; Heraclides is exiled.
359?	Dionysius II confiscates Dion's property and forces Arete to remarry.
ca. 357/6	Dion invades Sicily.
356	Dion withdraws to Leontini when the Syracusans prefer Heraclides, returns at the request of the Syracusans when Dionysius attacks Syracuse.
355?	Apollocrates surrenders Ortygia; Dion is reunited with his wife and son.
355?	Heraclides is murdered.
ca. 354/3	Dion is murdered.

Inppaurinus

Marriage?

Denis   Dionysius superior   — Arist   Dion

Dionysius
Jr.

        Hipp   Niscaeus Sophr. Arete

propinquitas, -tatis - nearness
                        relatedness

                generosam
                    high-born

                        fama - reputation
                        of his ancestors

- augeō, augére,
  auxī, auctum

ingenium, -ī (n.)
    nature

                    quas tyranni

affinitas, affinitatis - family
                        relation

    necessitudinis - family
                    necessi

1 DION, Hipparini filius, Syracusanus, nobili genere natus,
utraque implicatus tyrannide Dionysiorum. namque ille
superior Aristomachen, sororem Dionis, habuit in matri-
monio, ex qua duos filios, Hipparinum et Nisaeum,
procreavit totidemque filias, nomine Sophrosynen et Areten, 5
quarum priorem Dionysio filio, eidem cui regnum reliquit,
2 nuptum dedit, alteram, Areten, Dioni. Dion autem praeter
nobilem propinquitatem generosamque maiorum famam
multa alia ab natura habuit bona, in his ingenium docile,
come, aptum ad artes optimas, magnam corporis dignitatem, 10
quae non minimum commendat, magnas praeterea divitias
3 a patre relictas, quas ipse tyranni muneribus auxerat. erat
intimus Dionysio priori, neque minus propter mores quam
affinitatem. namque etsi Dionysii crudelitas ei displicebat,
tamen salvum propter necessitudinem, magis etiam suorum 15
causa studebat. aderat in magnis rebus, eiusque consilio
multum movebatur tyrannus, nisi qua in re maior ipsius
4 cupiditas intercesserat. legationes vero omnes, quae essent
illustriores, per Dionem administrabantur : quas quidem ille
diligenter obeundo, fideliter administrando crudelissimum 20
5 nomen tyranni sua humanitate leniebat. hunc a Dionysio
missum Karthaginienses suspexerunt, ut neminem umquam
Graeca lingua loquentem magis sint admirati.
2 Neque vero haec Dionysium fugiebant : nam quanto
esset sibi ornamento, sentiebat. quo fiebat ut uni huic 25
2 maxime indulgeret neque eum secus diligeret ac filium : qui
quidem, cum Platonem Tarentum venisse fama in Siciliam
esset perlata, adulescenti negare non potuerit, quin eum
accerseret, cum Dion eius audiendi cupiditate flagraret.
dedit ergo huic veniam magnaque eum ambitione Syracusas 30
3 perduxit. quem Dion adeo admiratus est atque adamavit,

8 generosam prop. nobilemque *Dederich*   11 commendat *Lamb.*:
commendatur *codd.*   21 leniebat *Lamb.*: tenebat *codd.*: tegebat
u et dett.   26 magis *A¹Ru et uar. lect. in P*

ut se ei totum traderet.   neque vero minus ipse Plato
delectatus est Dione.   itaque cum a Dionysio crudeliter
violatus esset, quippe quem venumdari iussisset, tamen
eodem rediit eiusdem Dionis precibus adductus.   interim in 4
5 morbum incidit Dionysius.   quo cum gravi conflictaretur,
quaesivit a medicis Dion, quem ad modum se haberet,
simulque ab iis petiit, si forte maiori esset periculo, ut sibi
faterentur :   nam velle se cum eo colloqui de partiendo
regno, quod sororis suae filios ex illo natos partem regni
10 putabat debere habere.   id medici non tacuerunt et ad 5
Dionysium filium sermonem rettulerunt.   quo ille commotus,
ne agendi esset Dioni potestas, patri soporem medicos dare
coegit.   hoc aeger sumpto ut somno sopitus diem obiit
supremum.

15   Tale initium fuit Dionis et Dionysii simultatis, eaque 3
multis rebus aucta est.   sed tamen primis temporibus
aliquamdiu simulata inter eos amicitia mansit.   cum Dion
non desisteret obscrare Dionysium, ut Platonem Athenis
arcesseret et eius consiliis uteretur, ille, qui in aliqua re
20 vellet patrem imitari, morem ei gessit.   eodemque tempore 2
Philistum historicum Syracusas reduxit, hominem amicum
non magis tyranno quam tyrannis.   sed de hoc in eo libro
plura sunt exposita, qui de historicis Graecis conscriptus est.
Plato autem tantum apud Dionysium auctoritate potuit 3
25 valuitque eloquentia, ut ei persuaserit tyrannidis facere finem
libertatemque reddere Syracusanis.   a qua voluntate Philisti
consilio deterritus aliquanto crudelior esse coepit.

    Qui quidem cum a Dione se superari videret ingenio, 4
auctoritate, amore populi, verens ne, si eum secum haberet,
30 aliquam occasionem sui daret opprimendi, navem ei trire-

---

1 ipse *Pu*: *om. rell.*   2 Dionysio] Dionysio tyranno *A^{1}u* :
tyranno *Nipp.*   3 quem] qui eum *Cobet*   13 aeger *ABRu* :
egit *P* : ergo *M*   sumpto ut (*om. M*) somno (sumno *Dan.* : sompno
P) *codd.* : ut somno *del. Nipp.*   22 quam tyrannidi *Ascensius*
in eo meo *ABMR*

mem dedit, qua Corinthum deveheretur, ostendens se id
utriusque facere causa, ne, cum inter se timerent, alteruter
2 alterum praeoccuparet. id cum factum multi indignarentur
magnaeque esset invidiae tyranno, Dionysius omnia, quae
moveri poterant Dionis, in navis imposuit ad eumque misit. 5
sic enim existimari volebat, id se non odio hominis, sed suae
3 salutis fecisse causa. postea vero quam audivit eum in
Peloponneso manum comparare sibique bellum facere
conari, Areten, Dionis uxorem, alii nuptum dedit filiumque
eius sic educari iussit, ut indulgendo turpissimis imbueretur 10
4 cupiditatibus. nam puero prius quam pubes esset scorta
adducebantur, vino epulisque obruebatur, neque ullum
5 tempus sobrio relinquebatur. is usque eo vitae statum
commutatum ferre non potuit, postquam in patriam rediit
pater (namque appositi erant custodes, qui eum a pristino 15
victu deducerent), ut se de superiore parte aedium deiecerit
atque ita interierit. sed illuc revertor.

5 Postquam Corinthum pervenit Dion et eodem perfugit
Heraclides ab eodem expulsus Dionysio, qui praefectus
fuerat equitum, omni ratione bellum comparare coeperunt. 20
2 sed non multum proficiebant, quod multorum annorum
tyrannus magnarum opum putabatur : quam ob causam
3 pauci ad societatem periculi perducebantur. sed Dion,
fretus non tam suis copiis quam odio tyranni, maximo animo
duabus onerariis navibus quinquaginta annorum imperium, 25
munitum quingentis longis navibus, decem equitum cen-
tumque peditum milibus, profectus oppugnatum, quod
omnibus gentibus admirabile est visum, adeo facile perculit,
ut post diem tertium, quam Siciliam attigerat, Syracusas
introierit. ex quo intellegi potest nullum esse imperium 30
4 tutum nisi benevolentia munitum. eo tempore aberat
Dionysius et in Italia classem opperiebatur adversariorum,

---

4 essent *AB*   22 tyrannis *Lamb.*   29 attigerat *Aldus* :
attigerit *codd.*

ratus neminem sine magnis copiis ad se venturum.   quae
res eum fefellit.   nam Dion iis ipsis, qui sub adversarii 5
fuerant potestate, regios spiritus repressit totiusque eius
partis Siciliae potitus est, quae sub Dionysii fuerat potestate,
5 parique modo urbis Syracusarum praeter arcem et insulam
adiunctam oppido, eoque rem perduxit, ut talibus pactioni- 6
bus pacem tyrannus facere vellet : Siciliam Dion obtineret,
Italiam Dionysius, Syracusas Apollocrates, cui maximam
fidem uni habebat Dion.

10   Has tam prosperas tamque inopinatas res consecuta est 6
subita commutatio, quod fortuna sua mobilitate, quem paulo
ante extulerat, demergere est adorta.   primum in filio, de 2
quo commemoravi supra, suam vim exercuit.   nam cum
uxorem reduxisset, quae alii fuerat tradita, filiumque vellet
15 revocare ad virtutem a perdita luxuria, accepit gravissimum
parens vulnus morte filii.   deinde orta dissensio est inter 3
eum et Heraclidem, qui, quod ei principatum non conce-
debat, factionem comparavit.   neque is minus valebat apud
optimates, quorum consensu praeerat classi, cum Dion
20 exercitum pedestrem teneret.   non tulit hoc animo aequo 4
Dion, et versum illum Homeri rettulit ex secunda rhapsodia,
in quo haec sententia est : non posse bene geri rem publicam
multorum imperiis.   quod dictum magna invidia consecuta
est : namque aperuisse videbatur omnia in sua potestate esse
25 velle.   hanc ille non lenire obsequio, sed acerbitate oppri- 5
mere studuit, Heraclidemque, cum Syracusas venisset,
interficiundum curavit.

Quod factum omnibus maximum timorem iniecit : nemo 7
enim illo interfecto se tutum putabat.   ille autem adversario
30 remoto, licentius eorum bona, quos sciebat adversus se
sensisse, militibus dispertivit.   quibus divisis cum cotidiani 2

    9 Dion] Dionysius *Lamb.* : *deleuit Heusinger* : *excidisse quaedam*
suspicatus est Nipp.   17 qui quod ei *Fleck.* : qui quod *R et Nipp.* :
qui quidem *codd.*   21 Homeri] homini *ABP*

maximi fierent sumptus, celeriter pecunia deesse coepit,
neque, quo manus porrigeret, suppetebat nisi in amicorum
possessiones. id eius modi erat, ut, cum milites recon-
3 ciliasset, amitteret optimates. quarum rerum cura frange-
batur et insuetus male audiendi non animo aequo ferebat, de 5
se ab iis male existimari, quorum paulo ante in caelum
fuerat elatus laudibus. vulgus autem offensa in eum
militum voluntate liberius loquebatur et tyrannum non
ferendum dictitabat.

8   Haec ille intuens cum quem ad modum sedaret nesciret 10
et quorsum evaderent timeret, Callicrates quidam, civis
Atheniensis, qui simul cum eo ex Peloponneso in Siciliam
venerat, homo et callidus et ad fraudem acutus, sine ulla
2 religione ac fide, adit ad Dionem et ait : eum magno in
periculo esse propter offensionem populi et odium militum, 15
quod nullo modo evitare posset, nisi alicui suorum negotium
daret, qui se simularet illi inimicum. quem si invenisset
idoneum, facile omnium animos cogniturum adversariosque
sublaturum, quod inimici eius dissidentis suos sensus aper-
3 turi forent. tali consilio probato excepit has partes ipse 20
Callicrates et se armat imprudentia Dionis. ad eum interficiundum socios conquirit, adversarios eius convenit, coniu-
4 ratione confirmat. res, multis consciis quae gereretur, elata
defertur ad Aristomachen, sororem Dionis, uxoremque
Areten. illae timore perterritae conveniunt, cuius de peri- 25
culo timebant. at ille negat a Callicrate fieri sibi insidias.
5 sed illa, quae agerentur, fieri praecepto suo. mulieres nihilo
setius Callicratem in aedem Proserpinae deducunt ac iurare
cogunt, nihil ab illo periculi fore Dioni. ille hac religione
non modo non est deterritus, sed ad maturandum concitatus 30
est, verens ne prius consilium aperiretur suum, quam conata
perfecisset.

    4 angebatur *Kellerbauer*   15 odio *A dell.*   19 dissidenti
Bremi   23 ageretur *Kellerbauer*

Hac mente proximo die festo, cum a conventu se remo- **9**
tum Dion domi teneret atque in conclavi edito recubuisset,
consciis facinoris loca munitiora oppidi tradit, domum cus-
todiis saepit, a foribus qui non discedant, certos praeficit,
5 navem triremem armatis ornat Philostratoque, fratri suo, **2**
tradit eamque in portu agitari iubet, ut si exercere remiges
vellet, cogitans, si forte consiliis obstitisset fortuna, ut haberet, qua fugeret ad salutem. suorum autem e numero **3**
Zacynthios adulescentes quosdam eligit cum audacissimos
10 tum viribus maximis, hisque dat negotium, ad Dionem eant
inermes, sic ut conveniendi eius gratia viderentur venire.
hi propter notitiam sunt intromissi. at illi ut limen eius **4**
intrarant, foribus obseratis in lecto cubantem invadunt,
colligant: fit strepitus, adeo ut exaudiri possit foris. hic, **5**
15 sicut ante saepe dictum est, quam invisa sit singularis
potentia et miseranda vita, qui se metui quam amari malunt, cuivis facile intellectu fuit. namque illi ipsi custodes, **6**
si propria fuissent voluntate, foribus effractis servare eum
potuissent, quod illi inermes telum foris flagitantes vivum
20 tenebant. cui cum succurreret nemo, Lyco quidam Syracusanus per fenestras gladium dedit, quo Dion inter-
fectus est.
    Confecta caede, cum multitudo visendi gratia introisset, **10**
nonnulli ab insciis pro noxiis conciduntur. nam celeri
25 rumore dilato, Dioni vim allatam, multi concurrerant, quibus
tale facinus displicebat. hi falsa suspicione ducti imme-
rentes ut sceleratos occidunt. huius de morte ut palam **2**
factum est, mirabiliter vulgi mutata est voluntas. nam qui
vivum eum tyrannum vocitarant, eidem liberatorem patriae
30 tyrannique expulsorem praedicabant. sic subito miseri-
cordia odio successerat, ut eum suo sanguine ab Acherunte, **3**
si possent, cuperent redimere. itaque in urbe celeberrimo
loco, elatus publice, sepulcri monumento donatus est. diem
obiit circiter annos LV natus, quartum post annum, quam
ex Peloponneso in Siciliam redierat.   **5**

Commentary

1.1 Dion: **Dion, Dionis,** 3rd declension. See **Introduction.**

Syracusanus: "of Syracuse"; adjective. Syracuse was founded by Greek colonists from Corinth in 734 B.C.

nobili genere natus: "born from a noble family"; ablative of origin with **natus** (< **nascor**).

utraque ... tyrannide: "in each tyranny," i.e., in both tyrannies.

Dionysiorum: Dionysius I, tyrant from 405 until his death in 367: Dionysius II succeeded his father, was driven out by Dion (357/6), and briefly returned to power in 347/6.

Aristomachen: < **Aristomache;** feminine accusative singular, formed as it would be in Greek; see also **Sophrosynen** and **Areten.**

eidem: < **idem.**

nuptum dedit: "he gave (to his son) to marry"; **nuptum** (< **nubo**) is accusative of the supine, used to express purpose, **AG** 509. Sophrosyne and Arete were Dion's nieces and Dionysius II's half-sisters. According to Plutarch (**Dion** 3) Dionysius I married Dionysius II's mother, Doris of Locri, and Aristomache at the same time.

1.2 maiorum: < **maiores,** here, as often, "ancestors."

in his: in = "among."

come: < **comis, come,** "courteous, companionable."

non minimum: "not the least," i.e., very much"; an example of litotes, the affirming of a thing by denying its contrary: **AG** 641.

auxerat: < **augeo;** "he had increased."
1.3   affinitatem: < **affinitas;** "relationship by marriage."

displicebat: < **displiceo,** "displease"; + dative.

salvum ... studebat: supply **esse:** "he was eager for him (Dionysius) to be secure."

necessitudinem: < **necessitudo;** "family relationship."

suorum causa: "for the sake of his own (family)."
multum: adverb.

qua in re: "in any matter"; **qui, qua (quae), quod,** the indefinite pronoun, here used as an adjective, occurs after **si, nisi, ne,** and **num,** AG 149.
1.4   vero: "but in fact"; adverb.

essent: subjunctive in a relative clause of characteristic, AG 534-535.

quas: "and ... these"; connecting relative; ˉ= **et has** and introduces the entire sentence, AG 308f.

obeundo [< **obeo**] **... administrando:** "by engaging in ... by performing"; gerunds.
1.5 Karthaginienses: "the Carthaginians"; < **Karthaginiensis.** Carthage was at this time the growing master of the Western Mediterranean. Some modern critics attribute the largely uninterrupted authoritarian rule at Syracuse and other Italo-Greek cities to pressures from Carthage.

Graeca lingua: ablative.

ut ... sint admirati: result clause; **admirati** is from **admiror.**

2.1   quanto ... sibi ornamento: "how great an asset to him"; double dative: dative of purpose (**quanto ... ornamento,** AG 382) and dative of reference (**sibi,** AG 367).

sibi: an indirect reflexive (**AG 300,2),** referring to Dionysius, the subject of **sentiebat.**

esset: subjunctive in the indirect question introduced by **quanto ... ornamento.**

quo: "and by this"; connecting relative.

fiebat: "it happened"; < **fio;** introduces a substantive clause of result (AG 367-368, note 2).

568

neque secus ... ac: "not otherwise than ... ";
with adjectives or adverbs of difference **ac (atque)** =
"than," **AG** 407d.

2.2 Platonem ... venisse: indirect statement dependent on **fama ... esse perlata.** Plato visited Tarentum
in 387 B.C.

Tarentum: accusative of place to which; the pre-
position is omitted before names of towns, cities, and
small islands.

potuerit: perfect subjunctive (the usual tense in
result clauses in secondary sequence, **AG** 485c); relative
clause of result with **qui** (= **ut is, AG** 537, 2).

quin ... accerseret: with **negare,** a verb of hin-
dering: "he (Dionysius) could not forbid the youth from
sending for him (Plato) ..."; **AG** 557-558, and note
examples in 558.

eius audiendi: "of (for) hearing him"; gerundive,
AG 503-504.

ambitione: < **ambitio,** "ostentation."

Syracusas: < **Syracusae, -arum;** see on
Tarentum above.

2.3 adeo: adverb, "so"; introduces a result clause.

delectatus est Dione: "he was delighted with
Dion."

quippe quem ... iussisset: quem = cum eum,
"since he had ordered him ..."; relative clause of
characteristic expressing cause, **AG** 535e, note 1; note
the change in subject between the main and subordinate
clauses.

eodem: "to the same place." Plato made two
more visits to Syracuse (soon after 367 and in 361); the
second of these occurred during Dion's exile in a vain
effort to have him recalled (Plato, **Seventh Letter**
327d-330c; 337e-350b).

2.4 quo ... gravi: sc. **morbo;** "by a serious one."

quaesivit a medicis ... ab iis petit: "asked from
the doctors ... asked from them," i.e., "asked them," **AG**
396a; **quaero** and **peto** may take indirect questions
(**quem ad modum**), or indirect commands (**ut
faterentur**), **AG** 563.

quem ad modum se haberet: "how he was."

forte: "by chance"; adverb.

velle se: implied indirect discourse; **se** refers to Dion.

2.5 **id:** object of **tacuerunt,** "kept quiet (about)."

ne ... esset Dioni: "so that Dion would not have"; purpose clause, **AG** 529-531; **Dioni** is dative of possession, AG 373; **potestas** is the subject.

soporem: < **sopor,** "sedative."

hoc ... sumpto: ablative absolute, AG 419.

ut somno sopitus: "as if lulled by sleep."

diem obiit supremum: "met his last day," i.e. died.

3.1 **simultatis:** < **simultas,** "rivalry."

non desisteret obsecrare: "did not stop beseeching."

uteretur: < **utor,** "use, make use of"; + ablative.

qui ... vellet: "since he wished"; relative clause expressing cause or motive (**qui** = **cum is**), AG 535e and 540c.

morem ei gessit: "humored him, complied with him."

3.2 **Philistum:** Under Dionysius II Philistus became admiral; he died when Heraclides defeated him at sea (356 B.C., Plutarch, **Dion** 35-36). Dionysius I had exiled Philistus, but according to Plutarch (**Dion** 11), Philistus had helped Dionysius I establish his tyranny, and had approved of tyranny in his history of Sicily, written during his banishment (compare **non magis tyranno quam tyrannis**). His history was admired in the late Roman Republic for its Thucydidean style.

libro: a lost portion of Nepos' **De viris illustribus.**

3.3 **auctoritate ... eloquentia:** ablatives of specification or respect, AG 418.

persuaserit ... facere: "persuaded to make"; **persuadeo** is usually constructed with **ut** + subjunctive (indirect command).

aliquanto: with **crudelior;** literally, "more cruel by somewhat," i.e., "somewhat more cruel"; ablative of degree of difference, AG 414.

4.1 Dion was exiled around 366 B.C.

ingenio, auctoritate, amore populi: ablative of specification or respect.

verens ne ... daret: "fearing that he would give." Verbs of fearing take a clause in the subjunctive; **ne** indicates affirmative, **ne non** or **ut**, the negative, **AG** ✳ **564.**

sui opprimendi: "an occasion for overthrowing him"; gerundive; **sui** refers to Dionysius.

navem ... triremem: "a ship with three banks of oars," i.e. a battleship; < **triremis,** adjective.

qua ... deveheretur: relative clause expressing purpose, **AG** 351, 2; see **AG** 533.

ostendens: "claiming."

utriusque ... causa: "for the sake of both."

inter se: i.e., "each other."

praeoccuparet: > **praeoccupo,** "anticipate, forestall."

4.2 **factum:** either a noun with **id;** "the deed"; or the perfect passive infinitive (with **esse** supplied), dependent on **indignarentur:** "they were indignant that it **(id)** had been done".

magnae ... tyranno: "it was a great (source of) unpopularity for the tyrant"; **magnae ... invidiae** is dative of purpose; **tyranno** is dative of reference.

ad eumque = **et ad eum;** writers generally do not attach **-que** to prepositions.

suae salutis: depends on **causa.**

4.3 **postea ... quam** = **posteaquam,** "after"; subordinating conjunction.

alii: dative < **alius.** In Plutarch's account Dion turned to war only after Dionysius dissolved his marriage to Arete (**Dion** 21-22).

4.4 **pubes:** "grown up, mature."

scorta: < **scortum,** "prostitute."

4.5 **usque eo:** "to the point that ..."; anticipates **ut ... deiecerit.**

aedium: < **aedes,** "chamber"; the plural ("rooms") = "house." See 8.4.

5.1 **eodem:** "to the same place"; adverb.

Heraclides: genitive **Heraclidis.** Dionysius exiled
him in 361 (Plato, **Third Letter** 318b-c and **Seventh
Letter** 348-349d). Plutarch maintains that Heraclides
quarreled with Dion and did not take part in the invasion, arriving in Syracuse after Dion's success (**Dion** 32).

omni ratione: "in every way."

5.2 **tyrannus ... putabatur:** supply **esse.**

magnarum opum [< ops]: "of great resources";
genitive of quality or description, **AG** 345.

quam ob causam: "and on account of this
reason"; connecting relative.

5.3 **sed Dion ... introierit:** Translate this long sentence as it comes, phrase by phrase and clause by clause.
Dion is the subject.

fretus: "relying upon"; + ablative.

maximo animo: "very courageously"; ablative of
manner.

duabus onerariis navibus: "with two freighters";
ablative of means.

imperium: accusative, direct object of both **oppugnatum** and **perculit.**

quingentis longis navibus: "with five hundred
warships"; ablative of means with **munitum.**

decem ... milibus: "with ten thousand"; + genitive **equitum (< eques)** "(of) horsemen"; ablative of
means.

centum: sc. **milibus.**

profectus: "having set out"; < **proficiscor;** modifies **Dion.**

oppugnatum: "to attack"; < **oppugno;** supine of
purpose.

quod ... est visum: "(a thing) that seemed"; par-
enthetical.

perculit: "he overthrew"; < **percello.**

post diem tertium quam: "the third day after";
post ... quam (= postquam) is a conjunction and
governs **attigerat.**

5.4 **ratus:** "having thought, thinking"; < **reor.**

fefellit: "deceived"; < **fallo.**

5.5 **iis ipsis:** "by the help of those very men"; mas-
culine ablative plural.

potitus est: "got possession of"; < **potior,** here + genitive, AG 410a (**partis** and **urbis**).

parique modo: "and in equal manner."

arcem [< arx] et insulam: The island, Ortygia, was the earliest inhabited site at Syracuse. It was joined to the mainland by a causeway, on which was the citadel (**arx**), and a bridge. Dionysius I had transformed Ortygia into an armed fortress for himself.

5.6 eoque rem perduxit ut: "and he brought the matter to the point (**eo,** "there") that ..."

talibus pactionibus: "on the following terms"; **talis,** as often, refers to what follows.

Siciliam ... Italiam ... Syracusas: Syracuse under Dionysius I had extended its influence throughout much of Sicily and into southern Italy (e.g., Locri and Rhegium). However, the "conditions" Nepos mentions were never agreed to by the Syracusans. Dionysius II secretly returned to Ortygia, but after failing to retake Syracuse, sailed back to Italy. Apollocrates surrendered Ortygia two years later (Plutarch, **Dion** 29, 37, 50.)

Apollocrates: son of Dionysius II; Dion's nephew.

cui ... uni: "in whom alone"; **uni** modifies **cui;** dative with **fidem ... habebat.**

6.1 paulo: "a little before"; ablative of degree of difference with **ante;** literally, "before by a little."

quem: "(the man) whom."

6.2 exercuit: fortuna is the subject.

fuerat tradita: pluperfect passive < **trado;** for **fuerat** instead of **erat** see AG p. 94, note 2.

6.3 praeerat: < **praesum,** "be in charge of"; + dative. Nepos is at odds here with Plutarch who locates Heraclides' support among the common people, not the aristocracy (**Dion** 32-33).

6.4 rhapsodia: "book." Nepos refers to **Iliad** 2.204, where the Greek says literally, "not a good thing is the rule of many; let there be one ruler."

aperuisse: "to have revealed"; < **aperio;** introduces indirect statement (**se**) ... **velle.**

6.5 hanc: refers to **invidia.**

interficiundum ... curavit: With the gerundive **curare** means "get/have something done"; so here "he had H. killed." On the form **interficiundum:** In gerundives of the third conjugation -u- sometimes appears instead of -e- (**AG** p. 89, note 1).

7.1   iniecit: < **inicio;** here with accusative and dative, **AG** 370.

7.2   pecunia: ablative of separation with **desum** (**AG** 400 and **AG** 401).

quo manus porrigeret suppetebat: Supply **locus** as subject for **suppetebat** and antecedent of **quo:** "nor was a place (source) available, where (**quo**) he might extend his hands ..."

id eius modi erat: "it was of that sort," i.e., "the situation was such"; **eius modi** is a genitive of quality.

reconciliasset: contracted pluperfect < **reconciliavisset.**

7.3   insuetus male audiendi: "unaccustomed to having a bad reputation"; **male audire** is an idiom, "hear evil (about oneself)," literally, "hear evilly."

existimari: The infinitive is direct object of **ferebat.**

fuerat elatus: pluperfect passive < **effero.** See on 6.2.

offensa ... voluntate: ablative absolute.

tyrannum non ferendum [esse]: "that the tyrant was not to be endured"; **ferendum (esse)** is the passive periphrastic (**AG** 196) in indirect statement.

8.1   quem ad modum: "how"; introduces indirect question.

quorsum: "in what direction"; adverb.

Callicrates: genitive **Callicratis;** Plutarch and Diodorus Siculus call him Callippus; Plato (**Seventh Letter**) locates C.'s friendship with Dion in their common experience of the Mysteries, a secret ritual practiced at Eleusis in which many Athenians were initiates; see on 8.5, **Proserpinae.**

adit ... ait: historical present; translate as past tenses. The sequence is secondary.

8.2 quod ... posset: A dependent clause in indirect discourse has a subjunctive verb if it is part of the reported statement, AG 580.

nisi ... daret: "if he did not give" (literally, "would not give"). In future conditions in indirect discourse (secondary sequence) the imperfect subjunctive is used for the future indicative of direct statement, AG 589a.3.

quem: See on 1.3.

si invenisset: "if he would find" (literally, "would have found"). In future conditions in indirect statement (secondary sequence) the pluperfect subjunctive is used for the future perfect indicative of direct statement, AG 589a.3.

sublaturum [esse]: "that he would destroy"; **sublaturum < tollo.**

eius: qualifies **inimici.**

dissidentis = dissidentes, accusative plural with **suos sensus.**

forent: instead of **essent;** see AG 170 for forms.

8.3 ad eum interficiundum: gerundive expressing purpose.

8.4 conveniunt ... timebant: Supply **eum** as direct object for **conveniunt** and as antecedent for **cuius:** "they meet the one for whose danger they fear."

8.5 nihilo setius: "nonetheless"; **setius** is comparative < **secus; nihilo** is ablative of degree of difference.

aedem: < aedes, -is, "chamber"; here, as often, the singular means "temple." See above on 4.5.

Proserpinae: Proserpina (Greek, Persephone) and her mother Ceres (Demeter) were the principal divinities worshipped in the Mysteries; since both Dion and Callicrates were initiates, an oath by Proserpina was probably the most binding the two women could think of.

periculi: partitive genitive with **nihil.**

fore = futurum esse, see AG 170a.

ad maturandum: "to haste"; literally, "to hastening, bringing to maturity."

prius ... quam = **priusquam**, subordinating conjunction.

conata: "attempts"; neuter plural accusative participle < **conor.**

9.1 hac mente: ablative of manner.

in conclavi edito: "in an upper room."

tradit: The implied subject is Callicrates.

foribus: "doors"; < **foris**, usually in plural.

qui ... discedant: relative clause of purpose; antecedent is **certos.**

9.2 ut si: "as if"; with subjunctive.

cogitans ... ut haberet: "planning that he would have"; **cogito** in this sense may take either the infinitive or **ut** + subjunctive.

si ... obstitisset: For condition see on 8.2; **obstitisset** < **obsto**, "stand in the way (of)"; + dative.

qua fugeret: "(a way) whereby he could flee."

9.3 Zacynthios: < **Zacynthius**, "Zacynthian." Zacynthus, an island off the western coast of Greece, was the rendezvous for Dion's invasion of Sicily (Plutarch, **Dion** 22); this perhaps accounts for the presence of Zacynthians among his trusted acquaintances.

cum ... tum: "not only ... but also."

eant: < **eo**; indirect command (**dat negotium**) without **ut**, AG 565a.

conveniendi eius gratia: "for the sake of meeting him"; **gratia** (ablative), like **causa**, expresses purpose with gerund or gerundive.

9.4 intrarant: contracted pluperfect < **intraverant.**

colligant: < **colligare**, "bind, stop."

9.5 foris: "outside"; adverb.

hic: "at this point, here"; adverb.

quam invisa sit: "how hateful is"; indirect question.

miseranda: sc. **quam**, "how pitiable."

qui ... malunt: supply **eorum** from the preceding clause to be the antecedent.

cuivis: < **quivis**, "anyone (you want)"; indefinite pronoun.

facile intellectu: "easy to understand"; supine in the ablative of respect with **facile, AG** 510, note 1.

si ... fuissent ... potuissent: "if they had been ... (they) would have been able"; past contrary-to-fact condition, **AG** 517.

propria ... voluntate: ablative of quality.

vivum: sc. Dionem, < **vivus.**

10.1 Dioni vim allatam: Supply **esse;** indirect statement dependent on **rumore dilato.** **Dioni** is dative with the compound verb **allatam** < **affero,** "bring to bear, use against."

concurrerant: pluperfect indicative.

ut sceleratos: "as if they were guilty."

10.2 ut palam factum est: "when it was made public."

vocitarant: contracted pluperfect < **vocitaverant.**

odio: dative with **succedo.**

Acherunte: < **Acheruns, Acheruntis** (archaic form of **Acheron, -ontis**), one of the rivers in Hades, i.e. death.

10.3 annos LV natus: "fifty-five years old."

quartum post annum quam: "four years after"; **postquam** is a subordinating conjunction.